OPTIONS TRADING

*Options Trading Demystified |
Profits, Risks, and Strategies*

Dominic Bates

OPTIONS TRADING
© Copyright 2023 by Dominic Bates
All rights reserved

This document is geared towards providing exact and reliable information with regards to the topic and issue covered. The publication is sold with the idea that the publisher is not required to render accounting, officially permitted, or otherwise, qualified services. If advice is necessary, legal or professional, a practiced individual in the profession should be ordered.

From a Declaration of Principles which was accepted and approved equally by a Committee of the American Bar Association and a Committee of Publishers and Associations.

In no way is it legal to reproduce, duplicate, or transmit any part of this document in either electronic means or in printed format. Recording of this publication is strictly prohibited and any storage of this document is not allowed unless with written permission from the publisher. All rights reserved.

The information provided herein is stated to be truthful and consistent, in that any liability, in terms of inattention or otherwise, by any usage or abuse of any policies, processes, or directions contained within is the solitary and utter responsibility of the recipient reader. Under no circumstances will any legal responsibility or blame be held against the publisher for any reparation, damages, or monetary loss due to the information herein, either directly or indirectly.

Respective authors own all copyrights not held by the publisher.

The information herein is offered for informational purposes solely, and is universal as so. The presentation of the information is without contract or any type of guarantee assurance.

The trademarks that are used are without any consent, and the publication of the trademark is without permission or backing by the trademark owner. All trademarks and brands within this book are for clarifying purposes only and are owned by the owners themselves, not affiliated with this document.

TABLE OF CONTENTS

Chapter 1: Introduction to Options Trading
    What Are Options?
    Why Trade Options?
    Types of Options

Chapter 2: Getting Started with Options
    Option Terminology
    Options vs. Stocks
    Options Trading Platforms

Chapter 3: Basic Option Strategies
    Buying Call Options
    Buying Put Options
    Covered Call Strategy

Chapter 4: Advanced Option Strategies
    Selling Covered Puts
    Iron Condor Strategy
    Butterfly Spread

Chapter 5: Option Pricing and Greeks
    Option Pricing Models
    Understanding Delta, Gamma, Theta, and Vega
    Implied Volatility

Chapter 6: Risk Management in Options Trading
    Position Sizing
    Stop Losses and Exit Strategies
    Margin and Leverage

Chapter 7: Options Trading Psychology
    Emotional Discipline

Managing Fear and Greed
Chapter 8: Trading Strategies and Techniques
　　　Swing Trading with Options
　　　Day Trading Options
　　　Long-Term Investing with Options
Chapter 9: Options Trading Tools and Resources
　　　Option Chains and Screeners
　　　Technical Analysis for Options
　　　Using Options for Income
Chapter 10: Case Studies and Real-Life Examples
　　　Case Study: Hedging a Stock Portfolio
　　　Real-Life Options Trading Success Stories
　　　　　Success Story 1: George Soros' Quantum Fund
　　　　　Success Story 2: Paul Tudor Jones and the 1987 Crash
　　　　　Success Story 3: Chris Sacca's Early Investment in Twitter
　　　Common Mistakes to Avoid
　　　　　Mistake 1: Neglecting Risk Management
　　　　　Mistake 2: Lack of Education and Planning
　　　　　Mistake 3: Emotional Trading
　　　　　Mistake 4: Neglecting Options Greeks
Chapter 11: Regulations and Taxes
　　　Taxation of Options Gains
　　　Regulatory Compliance
　　　Reporting Requirements
Chapter 12: The Future of Options Trading
　　　Innovations in Options Trading
　　　Cryptocurrency Options

Options Trading in a Changing Market
Chapter 13: Conclusion and Next Steps
Recap of Key Concepts
Creating Your Options Trading Plan
Continuing Your Options Trading Journey

Chapter 1: Introduction to Options Trading

Options trading is a financial instrument that has gained popularity in recent years, offering traders and investors a unique set of opportunities and risks. In this chapter, we will explore the fundamental concepts that form the bedrock of options trading.

What Are Options?

Options are financial contracts that give the holder the right, but not the obligation, to buy or sell an underlying asset at a predetermined price, known as the strike price, on or before a specified expiration date. These contracts are versatile and can be applied to a wide range of underlying assets, including stocks, commodities, currencies, and indices.

Key Characteristics of Options:

- **Call Options:** These give the holder the right to buy the underlying asset at the strike price.
- **Put Options:** These give the holder the right to sell the underlying asset at the strike price.
- **Expiration Date:** Options have a finite lifespan, and they expire on a specific date.
- **Strike Price:** The price at which the underlying asset can be bought or sold.
- **Premium:** The price paid to purchase the option contract.

Options offer flexibility and can be used for various purposes, including speculation, hedging, income generation, and risk management.

Why Trade Options?

Leveraged Returns:

One of the primary reasons traders are drawn to options is the potential for leveraged returns. With a relatively small investment (the premium), traders can control a much larger position in the underlying asset. This leverage magnifies both profits and losses, making options an attractive choice for those seeking high-risk, high-reward opportunities.

Risk Management:

Options also serve as valuable tools for risk management. Investors can use options to hedge their portfolios against adverse price movements in the underlying assets. For example, if you hold a portfolio of stocks, you can purchase put options to protect against a market downturn.

Income Generation:

Options can be used to generate income through strategies like covered call writing. In a covered call, an investor who owns the underlying asset sells call options against it, earning premiums in exchange for the potential obligation to sell the asset at a specified price.

Portfolio Diversification:

Options can provide a means of diversifying an investment portfolio. By incorporating options into a portfolio of traditional assets, investors can add another layer of risk management and profit potential.

Types of Options

There are two main types of options: call options and put options. These options can further be categorized into American options and European options based on when they can be exercised.

Call Options:

Call options give the holder the right to buy the underlying asset at the strike price. They are profitable when the price of the underlying asset rises above the strike price.

Put Options:

Put options give the holder the right to sell the underlying asset at the strike price. They are profitable when the price of the underlying asset falls below the strike price.

American Options:

American options can be exercised at any time before or on the expiration date. This flexibility can be advantageous, especially when the underlying asset's price is moving in a favorable direction.

European Options:

European options can only be exercised at the expiration date. While they offer less flexibility than American options, they can sometimes be less expensive due to their limited exercise window.

Chapter 2: Getting Started with Options

In this chapter, we will take the first steps into the world of options trading. It's important to build a solid foundation of understanding before diving into more complex strategies and concepts. Here, we will explore the key elements of options trading, starting with the essential terminology, followed by a comparison between options and stocks, and finally, a look at the various options trading platforms available.

Option Terminology

Options trading comes with its own set of jargon and terminology. Familiarizing yourself with these terms is crucial for effectively navigating the options market. Let's explore some of the fundamental terms you'll encounter:

- Strike Price:

The strike price is the pre-defined price at which the underlying asset can be bought (for call options) or sold (for put options). It plays a central role in determining the profitability of an option trade.

- Premium:

The premium is the price you pay to purchase an options contract. It represents the cost of acquiring the rights and potential obligations associated with the option.

- Expiration Date:

Options contracts have a limited lifespan, known as the expiration date. It specifies the date when the option contract becomes invalid.

- In the Money (ITM), At the Money (ATM), Out of the Money (OTM):

Options are categorized based on their relationship to the current market price of the underlying asset.

- **In the Money (ITM):** A call option with a strike price below the current asset price or a put option with a strike price above the current asset price.
- **At the Money (ATM):** An option with a strike price approximately equal to the current asset price.

- **Out of the Money (OTM):** A call option with a strike price above the current asset price or a put option with a strike price below the current asset price.

- Call and Put Options:

- **Call Options:** These give you the right to buy the underlying asset at the strike price.
- **Put Options:** These give you the right to sell the underlying asset at the strike price.

- Contract Size:

The contract size represents the quantity of the underlying asset associated with a single options contract. It varies depending on the asset type.

- Option Chain:

An option chain is a list of all available options contracts for a specific underlying asset, including their strike prices and expiration dates.

Options vs. Stocks

Understanding the differences between options and stocks is essential for making informed investment decisions. Let's explore some key distinctions:

- **Ownership vs. Rights:**

- **Stocks:** When you buy a stock, you become a partial owner of the company and share in its profits and losses.
- **Options:** Owning an options contract grants you rights but not ownership of the underlying asset.

- **Limited Risk vs. Unlimited Risk:**

- **Stocks:** Your risk when buying stocks is limited to the amount you invested.
- **Options:** Depending on the strategy, options trading can involve limited risk (the premium paid for the option) or unlimited risk, especially with certain advanced strategies.

- **Leverage:**

- **Stocks:** Typically, stocks are not leveraged, meaning you invest the full purchase amount.
- **Options:** Options provide built-in leverage, allowing you to control a larger position with a smaller investment.

Options Trading Platforms

Options trading platforms are the tools that enable you to execute your trades and manage your options positions. The choice of platform can significantly impact your trading experience. Here are some factors to consider:

- **Accessibility:**

Look for a platform that is user-friendly and offers a clear interface for placing and monitoring your trades.

- **Research Tools:**

A good platform should provide access to real-time market data, charts, and analytical tools to help you make informed decisions.

- **Commission and Fees:**

Understand the fee structure of the platform, including commissions, spreads, and any other charges.

- **Account Types:**

Different platforms may offer various types of accounts, such as cash accounts and margin accounts, each with its own features and requirements.

- **Customer Support:**

Reliable customer support is crucial for addressing any issues or questions you may have while trading.

- **Mobile Accessibility:**

Check whether the platform offers a mobile app for trading on the go.

Chapter 3: Basic Option Strategies

In this chapter, we will delve into the core concepts of basic option strategies. These strategies form the foundation of options trading and are essential for both beginners and experienced traders.

Buying Call Options

Buying call options is a straightforward strategy that allows traders to profit from upward price movements in an underlying asset. Here's how it works:

Step 1: Selecting an Underlying Asset: Begin by identifying an underlying asset (e.g., a stock) that you believe will increase in price.

Step 2: Choose a Call Option: Select a call option contract with a strike price that you expect the underlying asset to surpass before the option's expiration date.

Step 3: Pay the Premium: Pay the premium, which is the cost of purchasing the call option contract. This premium gives you the right to buy the underlying asset at the strike price, regardless of its current market price.

Step 4: Profit Potential: As the price of the underlying asset rises above the strike price, the value of your call option also increases. You can choose to sell the option for a profit or exercise it to buy the underlying asset at the strike price and then sell it at the current market price for a profit.

Risk: The risk in buying call options is limited to the premium paid. If the underlying asset's price does not rise above the strike price before expiration, the option may expire worthless, resulting in a loss of the premium.

Buying Put Options

Buying put options is the inverse of buying call options and is used to profit from downward price movements in an underlying asset. Here's how it works:

Step 1: Selecting an Underlying Asset: Identify an underlying asset that you believe will decrease in price.

Step 2: Choose a Put Option: Select a put option contract with a strike price that you expect the underlying asset to fall below before the option's expiration date.

Step 3: Pay the Premium: Pay the premium for the put option contract. This premium gives you the right to sell the underlying asset at the strike price, regardless of its current market price.

Step 4: Profit Potential: As the price of the underlying asset drops below the strike price, the value of your put option increases. You can sell the option for a profit or exercise it to sell the underlying asset at the strike price, which is higher than the market price, resulting in a profit.

Risk: The risk in buying put options is limited to the premium paid. If the underlying asset's price does not fall below the strike price before expiration, the option may expire worthless, resulting in a loss of the premium.

Covered Call Strategy

The covered call strategy combines stock ownership with call option writing to generate income. It is a conservative strategy used by investors seeking additional returns while holding a long position in an underlying asset. Here's how it works:

Step 1: Own the Underlying Asset: Start by owning the underlying asset, such as a stock.

Step 2: Write Call Options: Sell call options on the same underlying asset that you own. You specify a strike price and an expiration date for the call options.

Step 3: Collect Premium: Receive the premium paid by the call option buyer. This premium is income that you keep, regardless of what happens with the option.

Step 4: Risk and Profit: If the stock's price remains below the strike price, the call option expires worthless, and you keep the premium as profit. If the stock's price rises above the strike price, you may be obligated to sell your stock at the strike price, which can limit your potential gains but still result in a profit.

Risk: The primary risk in the covered call strategy is that the stock's price may increase significantly, causing you to miss out on potential gains above the strike price. However, you still profit from the premium received.

Chapter 4: Advanced Option Strategies

In this chapter, we will dive into advanced option strategies that offer more complexity and flexibility than basic strategies. These strategies require a deeper understanding of options and can be powerful tools for experienced traders. We will explore three advanced strategies: selling covered puts, the iron condor strategy, and the butterfly spread.

Selling Covered Puts

Selling covered puts is a strategy that allows traders to generate income by selling put options while simultaneously holding a short position in the underlying asset. This strategy is suitable for traders who are neutral to slightly bearish on the underlying asset's price. Here's how it works:

Step 1: Select an Underlying Asset: Choose an underlying asset that you believe will either remain stable or experience a slight decrease in price.

Step 2: Sell Put Options: Sell put options on the selected underlying asset. You will receive a premium for selling these options.

Step 3: Hold a Short Position: Ensure you have the means to buy the underlying asset at the put option's strike price in case you are assigned (required to fulfill the obligation).

Step 4: Collect Premium: You receive the premium from selling the put options as income.

Step 5: Profit Potential: If the underlying asset's price remains stable or rises, the put options expire worthless, and you keep the premium as profit. If the price drops below the strike price, you may be assigned to buy the asset at the strike price, but you still keep the premium received.

Risk: The main risk is that the underlying asset's price significantly decreases, and you are assigned to buy the asset at a higher price than its market value. However, the premium received helps offset potential losses.

Iron Condor Strategy

The iron condor strategy is a neutral strategy that profits from low volatility in the underlying asset's price. It involves selling both a call spread and a put spread on the same underlying asset. This strategy is designed to generate income while limiting potential losses. Here's how it works:

Step 1: Select an Underlying Asset: Choose an underlying asset with relatively low expected price volatility.

Step 2: Create a Call Spread: Sell an out-of-the-money (OTM) call option and simultaneously buy a higher OTM call option with a wider spread between them.

Step 3: Create a Put Spread: Sell an out-of-the-money put option and simultaneously buy a lower OTM put option with a wider spread between them.

Step 4: Collect Premium: You receive premiums from selling both the call and put options.

Step 5: Profit Potential: As long as the underlying asset's price remains within the range defined by the call and put spreads, all options expire worthless, and you keep the premiums as profit.

Risk: The risk in the iron condor strategy is that the underlying asset's price moves significantly beyond the defined range. If this happens, you may incur losses, but the premiums received help offset potential losses.

Butterfly Spread

The butterfly spread is a strategy that profits from low volatility and is used when you expect minimal price movement in the underlying asset. It involves using both call and put options to create a profit zone. Here's how it works:

Step 1: Select an Underlying Asset: Choose an underlying asset with expected low volatility.

Step 2: Create a Call Butterfly: Simultaneously buy an out-of-the-money (OTM) call option, sell two at-the-money (ATM) call options, and buy another OTM call option with a higher strike price. This creates a "winged" profit zone.

Step 3: Create a Put Butterfly: Repeat the process using put options, buying an OTM put, selling two ATM puts, and buying another OTM put with a lower strike price.

Step 4: Collect Premium: You receive premiums from selling the ATM call and put options, which help finance the purchase of the OTM options.

Step 5: Profit Potential: If the underlying asset's price remains within the "wings" of the butterfly spread, all options expire worthless, and you keep the premiums as profit.

Risk: The risk in the butterfly spread is that the underlying asset's price moves significantly beyond the "wings" of the spread, resulting in potential losses. However, the premiums received can help mitigate these losses.

In conclusion, these advanced option strategies offer traders more sophisticated ways to profit and manage risk in various market conditions. While they require a deeper understanding of options and a higher level of complexity, they can be powerful tools when used correctly. As you gain experience in options trading, consider incorporating these strategies into your trading toolbox to expand your opportunities and enhance your risk management capabilities.

Chapter 5: Option Pricing and Greeks

Understanding how options are priced and the factors that influence their value is essential for successful options trading. In this chapter, we will explore the intricacies of option pricing models, the Greek letters (Delta, Gamma, Theta, and Vega) that quantify an option's sensitivity to various factors, and the concept of implied volatility.

Option Pricing Models

Option pricing models are mathematical tools used to estimate the fair market value of options. Two primary models are widely used: the Black-Scholes model and the Binomial model.

- **Black-Scholes Model:**

Developed by economists Fischer Black, Myron Scholes, and Robert Merton in the early 1970s, the Black-Scholes model is a widely recognized option pricing model. It calculates the theoretical price of European-style options (options that can only be exercised at expiration) using variables such as the current stock price, strike price, time to expiration, implied volatility, and risk-free interest rate.

- **Binomial Model:**

The binomial model is a discrete-time model that breaks down the time to expiration into smaller intervals. It calculates option prices at each interval, making it particularly useful for American-style options (options that can be exercised at any time before expiration). The binomial model is conceptually simpler than the Black-Scholes model and can be valuable for options with complex features or early exercise possibilities.

Understanding Delta, Gamma, Theta, and Vega

The Greek letters Delta, Gamma, Theta, and Vega are used to quantify how an option's price changes in response to various factors:

- **Delta (Δ):**

Delta measures the sensitivity of an option's price to changes in the price of the underlying asset. It indicates how much an option's value is expected to change when the underlying asset's price moves by one point. For example, if an option has a delta of

0.50, its price is expected to increase by $0.50 for every $1 increase in the underlying asset's price, and vice versa.

- **Gamma (Γ):**

Gamma represents the rate of change of an option's delta. It measures how much an option's delta changes in response to a one-point change in the underlying asset's price. Gamma is crucial for assessing how delta will evolve as the underlying asset's price moves, especially for traders employing complex strategies.

- **Theta (Θ):**

Theta measures the rate of time decay of an option's value. It indicates how much an option's price is expected to decrease as time passes, assuming all other factors remain constant. Theta highlights the erosion of an option's value as it approaches its expiration date, making it important for traders who use time-sensitive strategies like selling options.

- **Vega (v):**

Vega quantifies an option's sensitivity to changes in implied volatility. It represents the expected change in an option's price for a one-point change in implied volatility. High vega options are more sensitive to changes in volatility, making them appealing for traders who anticipate increased market turbulence.

Implied Volatility

Implied volatility is a critical concept in options trading. It represents the market's consensus on the future volatility of the underlying asset and is not necessarily tied to historical volatility. When implied volatility increases, option prices tend to rise, and when it decreases, option prices tend to fall.

Traders often use implied volatility to assess whether options are overvalued or undervalued relative to historical volatility. High implied volatility can present opportunities for option buyers looking for increased price movement, while option sellers may benefit from selling options when implied volatility is high and expected to decline.

Chapter 6: Risk Management in Options Trading

Effective risk management is a cornerstone of successful options trading. In this chapter, we will explore essential risk management techniques that every options trader should understand and implement. These techniques include position sizing, stop losses and exit strategies, and considerations related to margin and leverage.

Position Sizing

Position sizing is the process of determining the number of options contracts or shares of an underlying asset to trade in each position. Proper position sizing is critical to control risk and protect your trading capital. Here are key principles to consider:

- **Risk Percentage:**

Determine the maximum percentage of your trading capital that you are willing to risk on a single trade. A common guideline is to risk no more than 1-2% of your total trading capital on any given trade.

- **Volatility Assessment:**

Consider the volatility of the underlying asset and the options you are trading. Highly volatile assets may require smaller position sizes to accommodate price swings.

- **Stop Loss Placement:**

Set stop loss orders to limit potential losses. Your position size should align with the distance between your entry point and stop loss level. A smaller stop loss may allow for a larger position size, and vice versa.

- **Portfolio Diversification:**

Diversify your positions across different assets and strategies to reduce the impact of a single losing trade on your overall portfolio.

Stop Losses and Exit Strategies

Stop losses and exit strategies are essential tools for managing risk and preserving capital. They help you exit trades when they are not going as planned. Consider the following techniques:

- **Hard Stop Loss:**

Place a hard stop loss order with your broker at a predetermined price level. This order automatically exits your position if the underlying asset's price reaches the specified level. Hard stop losses are crucial for limiting losses and preventing emotional decision-making.

- Trailing Stop:

A trailing stop moves with the market price. If the asset's price moves in your favor, the stop loss adjusts to lock in profits. Trailing stops are useful for capturing gains while still protecting against adverse price movements.

- Time-Based Exits:

Set predefined time limits for your trades. If a trade does not reach your target within a specified time frame, consider exiting to free up capital for better opportunities.

- **Profit Targets:**

Determine profit targets based on technical analysis or your trading strategy. When your position reaches the target, consider taking profits to secure gains.

Margin and Leverage

Margin and leverage are double-edged swords in options trading. While they can amplify gains, they also increase the potential for losses. Here's what you need to know:

- **Margin Trading:**

Margin trading allows you to control a larger position with a smaller amount of capital. However, it also exposes you to the risk of losing more than your initial investment. Understand your broker's margin requirements and use margin cautiously.

- **Leverage:**

Leverage magnifies both profits and losses. High leverage can quickly deplete your trading capital if a trade goes against you. Ensure that you are aware of the leverage effect when choosing your position size.

- **Margin Calls:**

Brokers issue margin calls when your account balance falls below a certain threshold due to losses. To avoid margin calls, maintain a buffer of capital in your account, and monitor your positions regularly.

- Risk of Assignment:

When you sell options, particularly naked options, you may be at risk of assignment. Understand the potential obligations and risks associated with your options positions and have a plan in place to manage them.

In conclusion, risk management is paramount in options trading. Position sizing, stop losses, and exit strategies help protect your capital and limit losses. Understanding the implications of margin and leverage is essential for making informed decisions. By implementing effective risk management techniques, you can navigate the complexities of options trading with greater confidence and discipline, increasing your chances of long-term success in the markets.

Chapter 7: Options Trading Psychology

Options trading is not just about understanding strategies and market analysis; it also heavily relies on mastering the psychological aspects of trading. In this chapter, we will delve into the crucial elements of options trading psychology, including emotional discipline, managing fear and greed, and cultivating the right trading mindset.

Emotional Discipline

Emotional discipline is the ability to remain calm, rational, and in control of your emotions while trading. It is a fundamental trait for successful options traders. Here are some strategies to cultivate emotional discipline:

- **Develop a Trading Plan:**

Create a detailed trading plan that outlines your objectives, strategies, risk tolerance, and rules for entering and exiting trades. A well-defined plan can help you stay focused and reduce impulsive decisions.

- **Risk Management:**

Implement sound risk management techniques, including position sizing and stop losses, to limit potential losses. Knowing that you have a safety net in place can alleviate anxiety and impulsive actions.

- **Stay Informed, but Avoid Overanalysis:**

Stay informed about market developments, but be cautious not to overanalyze. Too much information can lead to analysis paralysis and emotional stress. Stick to your plan and avoid making impulsive decisions based on news or rumors.

- **Practice Patience:**

Options trading often requires patience. Avoid the urge to chase quick profits or revenge trade after a loss. Patience allows you to wait for the right setups and opportunities.

Managing Fear and Greed

Fear and greed are two powerful emotions that can influence trading decisions. Managing these emotions is crucial for maintaining consistency and avoiding impulsive actions:

- **Fear:**
  - **Identify Your Fears:** Recognize specific fears that affect your trading, such as the fear of losing money or the fear of missing out (FOMO).

- **Risk Tolerance**: Determine your risk tolerance and stick to it. If a trade makes you excessively anxious, it may be too large for your comfort level.
- **Mindfulness Techniques:** Use mindfulness techniques, such as deep breathing and visualization, to manage fear during stressful trading situations.

- Greed:

- **Set Realistic Goals:** Set achievable profit targets and avoid setting overly ambitious expectations. Greed can lead to overtrading or holding positions for too long, hoping for larger profits.
- **Take Profits:** When a trade reaches your profit target, consider taking at least a portion of the profits off the table. This can help counteract the temptation to become overly greedy.

7.3 Trading Mindset

Developing the right trading mindset is an ongoing process that can significantly impact your success as an options trader:

- **Positive Self-Talk:**

    - **Challenge Negative Beliefs:** Identify and challenge negative self-talk or limiting beliefs about your trading abilities. Replace them with positive and empowering thoughts.
    - **Maintain Confidence:** Confidence in your trading strategy and abilities is essential. Confidence allows you to stick with your plan even during challenging times.

- **Resilience:**

    - **Accepting Losses:** Understand that losses are a part of trading. A resilient mindset helps you bounce back from losses and stay committed to your trading plan.

- **Continuous Learning:**

  - **Stay Open to Learning:** The markets are constantly evolving. A growth mindset that embraces continuous learning and adaptation is crucial for long-term success.

- **Stay Disciplined:**

  - **Consistency:** Maintain discipline by following your trading plan consistently. Avoid impulsive deviations from your strategy.

By focusing on these psychological elements, you can enhance your decision-making, maintain consistency, and navigate the challenges of the options market with greater confidence and resilience.

Chapter 8: Trading Strategies and Techniques

In this chapter, we will explore various trading strategies and techniques involving options. Whether you prefer to swing trade, day trade, or take a long-term investment approach, there are options strategies to suit your trading style and objectives. We will delve into swing trading with options, day trading options, and long-term investing with options.

Swing Trading with Options

Swing trading is a strategy that aims to capture short to medium-term price swings in the market. It involves holding positions for several days to weeks to profit from both upward and downward price movements. Options can be particularly useful for swing trading due to their flexibility and limited risk. Here's how to swing trade with options:

- **Identify Swing Opportunities:**

Look for stocks or underlying assets that are exhibiting price patterns or trends suitable for swing trading. This may involve technical analysis to identify potential entry and exit points.

- **Select Options Contracts:**

Choose options contracts with expiration dates that align with your swing trading timeframe. Consider using at-the-money (ATM) or slightly out-of-the-money (OTM) options for flexibility.

- **Set Entry and Exit Rules:**

Establish clear entry and exit rules based on your analysis. This includes setting profit targets and stop losses to manage risk.

- Manage Risk:

Position sizing and risk management are crucial. Ensure you only risk a small percentage of your trading capital on each trade, and use stop-loss orders to limit potential losses.

- Review and Adjust:

Continuously monitor your swing trades and be prepared to adjust your strategy based on changing market conditions.

Day Trading Options

Day trading involves opening and closing positions within the same trading day, aiming to profit from intraday price fluctuations. While day trading options can be challenging due to the rapid price movements, it can also be rewarding. Here are steps to day trade options effectively:

- **Select Highly Liquid Options:**

Opt for options contracts with high liquidity and tight bid-ask spreads to ensure efficient execution.

- **Develop a Trading Plan:**

Create a detailed trading plan that includes specific entry and exit criteria, position sizing, and risk management rules.

- **Monitor Market Volatility:**

Be aware of overall market volatility and news events that could impact your trades. Volatility can present both opportunities and risks for day traders.

- **Use Technical Analysis:**

Employ technical analysis techniques, such as chart patterns and indicators, to identify potential entry and exit points.

- **Manage Risk:**

Set strict stop-loss orders to limit potential losses and stick to your risk management plan. Day trading can be high-paced and emotional, so discipline is essential.

Long-Term Investing with Options

Options are not only for short-term trading; they can also be employed in a long-term investment strategy. Long-term investing with options involves using options to enhance returns, protect against downside risk, or generate income over an extended period. Here's how to approach long-term investing with options:

- **Covered Call Writing:**

One common long-term strategy is to own a portfolio of stocks and periodically sell covered call options against those stocks to generate income.

- **Protective Puts:**

Invest in a protective put strategy where you buy long-dated put options to protect your portfolio against significant market declines.

- **LEAPS (Long-Term Equity Anticipation Securities):**

Consider using LEAPS, which are long-term call or put options with expiration dates extending up to several years. LEAPS provide flexibility for long-term investors to participate in price movements.

- Income Generation:

Explore income-generating strategies, such as cash-secured puts or credit spreads, to generate consistent returns over time.

- Regular Portfolio Review:

Continuously assess your long-term options strategies in conjunction with your overall investment portfolio. Adjust as needed based on changing market conditions and your financial goals.

In conclusion, options provide a wide range of strategies and techniques for traders and investors, catering to various trading styles and timeframes.

Whether you prefer swing trading, day trading, or a long-term investment approach, options can be a valuable tool for achieving your financial objectives. However, remember that options trading involves risks, and it's essential to have a clear strategy, risk management plan, and discipline in your trading or investment activities.

Chapter 9: Options Trading Tools and Resources

Successful options trading requires access to the right tools and resources. In this chapter, we will explore essential options trading tools and resources that can enhance your decision-making, improve your strategies, and help you navigate the complex world of options trading. These resources include option chains and screeners, technical analysis for options, and using options for income.

Option Chains and Screeners

Option chains and screeners are valuable tools for identifying potential options trades and conducting research on available options contracts.

- **Option Chains:**

Option chains provide a visual representation of available options contracts for a specific underlying asset. They list various strike prices and expiration dates for both calls and puts. Traders can use option chains to compare premiums, assess liquidity, and evaluate potential trades.

- Option Screeners:

Option screeners are powerful tools that allow traders to filter and search for specific options contracts that meet predefined criteria. These criteria can include volume, open interest, implied volatility, and more. Option screeners help traders identify potential trading opportunities based on their strategies and preferences.

- Research and Analysis:

Utilize option chains and screeners to conduct in-depth research and analysis. Examine historical options data, implied volatility trends, and pricing information to make informed decisions.

Technical Analysis for Options

Technical analysis is a valuable tool for evaluating options and making trading decisions. It involves studying historical price and volume data to predict future price movements. Here's how technical analysis can be applied to options:

- Chart Patterns:

Identify chart patterns, such as support and resistance levels, trendlines, and reversal patterns, to make entry and exit decisions. Patterns can provide insights into potential price direction.

- Indicators and Oscillators:

Use technical indicators and oscillators, such as moving averages, Relative Strength Index (RSI), and

MACD, to assess the strength and momentum of price movements. These tools can help confirm or challenge trading signals.

- **Volatility Analysis:**

Analyze historical volatility and implied volatility levels to gauge the potential risk and reward of options positions. Volatility can significantly impact option premiums.

- **Risk Management:**

Incorporate technical analysis into your risk management strategy. For example, use technical indicators to set stop loss levels and exit points for options trades.

Using Options for Income

Options can be powerful tools for generating income in addition to capital appreciation. Here are ways to use options for income:

- **Covered Calls:**

Sell covered call options against stocks you own. By doing so, you collect premiums, which can serve as income. If the options expire worthless, you keep the premium and the underlying stock.

- **Cash-Secured Puts:**

Sell cash-secured put options. This strategy obligates you to buy the underlying asset at the strike price if assigned. In exchange, you receive a premium. If not assigned, you keep the premium as income.

- **Credit Spreads:**

Employ credit spreads, such as bull put spreads or bear call spreads, to collect premiums. These strategies involve selling one option and buying another with a different strike price to limit risk.

- **Dividend Capture with Covered Calls:**

Use covered calls to capture dividends. Sell covered calls on stocks just before their ex-dividend dates to receive the dividend income while still generating premium income.

- Income-Focused Strategies:

Explore income-focused options strategies, such as the Iron Condor or the Iron Butterfly, designed to generate income while managing risk.

Options trading tools and resources play a significant role in your success as an options trader. By leveraging these tools and resources effectively, you can become a more informed and strategic options trader, ultimately increasing your chances of achieving your financial goals in the options market.

Chapter 10: Case Studies and Real-Life Examples

In this chapter, we will delve into practical case studies and real-life examples that provide insights into options trading strategies, successes, and common pitfalls. By examining these real-world scenarios, you can gain a deeper understanding of how options can be applied effectively and avoid common mistakes.

Case Study: Hedging a Stock Portfolio

Scenario:

Imagine you have a well-diversified stock portfolio worth $500,000. You've been monitoring the market, and you're concerned about a potential downturn. To protect your portfolio from losses, you decide to implement a hedging strategy using options.

Strategy:

To hedge your stock portfolio, you choose to buy put options on a broad market index, such as the S&P 500. Here's how the strategy works:

Calculate the approximate value of your portfolio's beta, which represents its sensitivity to market movements.

Based on your portfolio's beta and desired level of protection, determine the number of put options to purchase.

Purchase long-dated put options on the S&P 500. These options will increase in value if the market declines, offsetting losses in your portfolio.

Result:

The stock market experiences a significant downturn, causing your stock portfolio to decline in value. However, the put options on the S&P 500 increase in value, providing a hedge against the losses in your portfolio. As a result, your overall net worth is better protected than if you had not employed the hedging strategy.

Real-Life Options Trading Success Stories

Success Story 1: George Soros' Quantum Fund

In the early 1990s, George Soros and his Quantum Fund made headlines by shorting the British pound (GBP) in a trade known as "Black Wednesday." Soros correctly predicted that the pound was overvalued within the European Exchange Rate Mechanism (ERM). The Quantum Fund used put options and futures contracts to profit from the pound's devaluation, earning approximately $1 billion in a single trade.

Success Story 2: Paul Tudor Jones and the 1987 Crash

Paul Tudor Jones, a prominent hedge fund manager, successfully anticipated the 1987 stock market crash. He used put options to protect his portfolio and profited from the market decline. Jones' fund gained about 200% during the crash, solidifying his reputation as a skilled trader.

Success Story 3: Chris Sacca's Early Investment in Twitter

Venture capitalist Chris Sacca made a savvy options trade by purchasing Twitter call options before the company's IPO. Sacca correctly anticipated Twitter's stock price would rise after the IPO. When Twitter's stock soared, his call options yielded substantial profits, showcasing the potential of options for speculating on stock price movements.

Common Mistakes to Avoid

Mistake 1: Neglecting Risk Management

One of the most common mistakes in options trading is failing to implement proper risk management. Traders may overleverage their positions, ignore stop-loss orders, or not diversify their strategies, leading to significant losses.

Mistake 2: Lack of Education and Planning

Jumping into options trading without sufficient education and planning is a recipe for disaster. It's essential to understand options thoroughly, develop a clear trading plan, and practice in a simulated environment before risking real capital.

Mistake 3: Emotional Trading

Emotional decision-making, driven by fear or greed, can lead to impulsive actions and poor results. Successful options traders maintain emotional discipline, stick to their trading plans, and avoid making rash decisions.

Mistake 4: Neglecting Options Greeks

Options traders often overlook the importance of options Greeks (Delta, Gamma, Theta, Vega). These measures provide critical insights into how options will behave under different market conditions. Neglecting them can lead to suboptimal trading strategies.

Chapter 11: Regulations and Taxes

Options trading is subject to regulations and tax implications that traders must understand and comply with. In this chapter, we will explore the taxation of options gains, the importance of regulatory compliance, and reporting requirements associated with options trading.

Taxation of Options Gains

Options trading can have tax consequences that vary depending on your country of residence and the specific type of options transactions you engage in. Here are some key considerations related to the taxation of options gains:

- **Capital Gains Tax:**

In many countries, gains from options trading are typically treated as capital gains. Capital gains tax rates may vary depending on whether the gains are short-term (held for a year or less) or long-term (held for more than a year). It's crucial to understand your country's tax laws and rates.

- **Options Expiration:**

The tax treatment of options gains may differ based on whether options contracts are exercised or allowed to expire. Exercised options may trigger taxable events, while expired options may not.

- **Reporting Requirements:**

Keep detailed records of your options transactions, including dates, strike prices, premiums, and outcomes. Accurate record-keeping is essential for calculating and reporting gains and losses on your tax returns.

- **Tax-Advantaged Accounts:**

Some countries offer tax-advantaged accounts, such as Individual Retirement Accounts (IRAs) in the United States. Options trading within these accounts may have different tax implications. Consult a tax professional to understand the specifics.

Regulatory Compliance

Compliance with regulations is vital to ensure that your options trading activities are legal and transparent. Regulatory bodies, such as the U.S. Securities and Exchange Commission (SEC) and the Financial Industry Regulatory Authority (FINRA), oversee options trading in many jurisdictions. Here's why regulatory compliance is crucial:

- **Investor Protection:**

Regulatory bodies aim to protect investors by ensuring that options markets operate fairly and transparently. Compliance with regulations helps maintain market integrity.

- Licensing and Registration:

Depending on your country and the type of options trading you engage in, you may be required to obtain licenses or register with relevant regulatory authorities. Failure to do so could result in legal consequences.

- Broker Regulation:

Ensure that your options broker is regulated by the appropriate authorities. Reputable brokers should be transparent about their regulatory status.

- Anti-Money Laundering (AML) and Know Your Customer (KYC) Requirements:

Be prepared to provide identification and financial information to your broker, as required by AML and KYC regulations. This helps prevent illegal activities like money laundering.

Reporting Requirements

Options traders may have reporting requirements related to their trading activities. These requirements can vary by jurisdiction and the volume of trading. Common reporting obligations include:

- Tax Reporting:

As mentioned earlier, options gains and losses should be accurately reported on your tax returns. Failure to report accurately can result in penalties or legal issues.

- Account Statements:

Your broker will provide periodic account statements that detail your options transactions. Review these statements for accuracy and retain them for your records.

- Regulatory Filings:

Depending on your jurisdiction and trading volume, you may be required to submit regulatory filings or reports to comply with local regulations. It's essential to understand your specific reporting obligations.

- **Income and Capital Gains Reporting:**

Different types of options strategies (e.g., covered calls, cash-secured puts) may have distinct tax treatment. Be aware of the specific reporting requirements for each strategy.

In conclusion, options trading involves navigating both regulatory and tax considerations. Understanding the taxation of options gains, complying with regulations, and meeting reporting requirements are essential aspects of responsible options trading. Consult with tax professionals and stay informed about the rules and regulations in your jurisdiction to ensure that your options trading activities are both legal and financially sound.

Chapter 12: The Future of Options Trading

The world of options trading is constantly evolving, driven by technological advancements, changing market dynamics, and new financial instruments. In this chapter, we will explore the future of options trading, including innovations in options trading, the emergence of cryptocurrency options, and the challenges and opportunities in a changing market landscape.

Innovations in Options Trading

The future of options trading is marked by ongoing innovations that aim to improve accessibility, efficiency, and risk management for traders. Here are some notable innovations to watch for:

- **Electronic Trading Platforms:**

Electronic options trading platforms have revolutionized the industry, offering real-time trading, advanced analytics, and increased transparency. As technology continues to advance, these platforms will become even more sophisticated.

- **Algorithmic Trading and AI:**

Algorithmic trading and artificial intelligence (AI) are playing a growing role in options trading. AI-driven algorithms can analyze vast amounts of data and execute trades at lightning speed, potentially leading to more efficient and profitable strategies.

- **Blockchain Technology:**

Blockchain technology has the potential to enhance the transparency and security of options trading. Smart contracts on blockchain platforms can automate aspects of options trading, reducing the need for intermediaries.

- **Options on Non-Traditional Assets:**

The expansion of options trading to non-traditional assets, such as commodities, cryptocurrencies, and environmental credits, opens up new opportunities for diversification and risk management.

Cryptocurrency Options

The rise of cryptocurrencies has given birth to a new frontier in options trading—cryptocurrency options. These financial derivatives allow traders to speculate on the price movements of cryptocurrencies like Bitcoin and Ethereum. Here's what you need to know about cryptocurrency options:

- **Volatility Opportunities:**

Cryptocurrency markets are known for their high volatility. Cryptocurrency options provide a way to profit from these price swings, whether through buying call options to speculate on rising prices or buying put options to hedge against declines.

- Liquidity and Exchange Options:

Major cryptocurrency exchanges now offer options trading alongside spot trading. This has improved liquidity and accessibility for traders looking to enter the cryptocurrency options market.

- Risk Management:

Cryptocurrency options can be used for risk management in crypto portfolios. Traders and investors can employ strategies like covered calls and protective puts to safeguard their cryptocurrency holdings.

- Regulation and Security:

The regulatory environment for cryptocurrency options is evolving. Traders should be cautious and select reputable exchanges that prioritize security and compliance.

Options Trading in a Changing Market

The future of options trading will also be influenced by changing market conditions and macroeconomic factors. Here are some considerations for options traders in a dynamic market environment:

- Geopolitical Events:

Geopolitical events, such as trade tensions, elections, and global conflicts, can have a significant impact on financial markets and options prices. Traders should stay informed and adapt their strategies accordingly.

- Market Volatility:

Market volatility, driven by economic data releases, corporate earnings reports, and unforeseen events, will continue to create opportunities and risks for options traders.

- Environmental and ESG Considerations:

Environmental, Social, and Governance (ESG) factors are increasingly influencing investment decisions. Options traders may need to incorporate ESG considerations into their strategies, especially as ESG-focused options products become available.

- Market Structure Changes:

Ongoing changes in market structure, including the role of high-frequency trading and the evolution of options market makers, can impact options liquidity and pricing.

The future of options trading holds exciting opportunities and challenges. Traders and investors who adapt to changes, stay informed, and employ effective risk management strategies are likely to thrive in the evolving world of options trading.

Chapter 13: Conclusion and Next Steps

Congratulations on completing this comprehensive guide to options trading! In this final chapter, we will recap key concepts, guide you in creating your options trading plan, and suggest next steps to continue your options trading journey.

Recap of Key Concepts

Throughout this guide, you've gained insights into various aspects of options trading. Let's recap some key concepts:

- What Are Options?

Options are financial derivatives that provide the right, but not the obligation, to buy (call) or sell (put) an underlying asset at a specified price (strike price) within a predetermined time frame (expiration date).

- Types of Options

There are two primary types of options: call options, which give the holder the right to buy an underlying asset, and put options, which give the holder the right to sell an underlying asset.

- Options Trading Strategies

Options trading offers a wide range of strategies, including buying and selling call and put options, covered calls, credit spreads, and more. Each strategy serves specific objectives and risk profiles.

- Options Pricing and Greeks

Understanding options pricing models and the Greeks (Delta, Gamma, Theta, Vega) is crucial for evaluating and managing options positions.

- Risk Management

Effective risk management, including position sizing, stop losses, and portfolio diversification, is essential for protecting your capital in options trading.

- **Psychology of Options Trading**

Mastering emotional discipline, managing fear and greed, and cultivating the right trading mindset are vital aspects of successful options trading.

- **Regulations and Taxes**

Complying with regulatory requirements and understanding the taxation of options gains is essential for responsible options trading.

Creating Your Options Trading Plan

As you conclude this guide, it's time to consider creating your options trading plan. A well-defined trading plan provides structure and discipline to your trading activities. Here are steps to help you create your plan:

- **Define Your Objectives:**

Start by setting clear and realistic objectives. What do you want to achieve through options trading? Are you looking for income, capital appreciation, or risk management?

- **Risk Tolerance:**

Assess your risk tolerance. How much capital are you willing to risk on each trade? What is your overall risk tolerance for your options trading portfolio?

- **Strategy Selection:**

Choose options trading strategies that align with your objectives and risk tolerance. Consider the strategies you've learned in this guide and select those that suit your preferences.

- **Trading Rules:**

Establish specific trading rules, including entry and exit criteria, position sizing guidelines, and risk management parameters.

- **Monitoring and Review:**

Implement a process for monitoring your trades and reviewing your trading plan regularly. Be prepared to adapt and refine your plan as needed.

- **Education and Resources:**

Continue your options trading education. Stay updated on market developments, options strategies, and risk management techniques.

Continuing Your Options Trading Journey

Options trading is a dynamic and evolving field. To continue your options trading journey and refine your skills, consider the following steps:

- **Paper Trading:**

Practice your options trading strategies in a simulated environment before risking real capital. Paper trading allows you to gain experience without financial risk.

- **Advanced Strategies:**

Explore more advanced options trading strategies as you become more experienced. These may include iron condors, butterflies, and straddles.

- **Stay Informed:**

Keep yourself informed about market news, economic events, and changes in market conditions that could impact your options trades.

- **Risk Management Mastery:**

Continue to refine your risk management techniques and adapt them to different market scenarios.

- **Mentorship and Communities:**

Consider joining options trading communities or seeking mentorship from experienced traders. Learning from others can accelerate your growth as a trader.

- Diversify and Adapt:

Explore options on different asset classes, including equities, commodities, and cryptocurrencies. Diversifying your options trading portfolio can enhance your risk-adjusted returns.

In conclusion, options trading offers a world of possibilities for traders and investors. By understanding the key concepts, creating a solid trading plan, and continuing your education and practice, you can embark on a rewarding options trading journey. Remember that options trading carries risks, and success often requires patience, discipline, and continuous learning. With dedication and the right approach, you can achieve your financial goals through options trading.

Milton Keynes UK
Ingram Content Group UK Ltd.
UKHW020733161023
430697UK00016B/748